Living Shambavism

A Year of Inner Practice Volume I

[ARRIVING]

A year of quiet companionship, remembering what has never been absent.

SHREE SHAMBAV

Living Shambavism
A Year of Inner Practice Volume One
Shree Shambav

Published by Shree Shambav, Tamil Nadu, India

First Edition, 2026

ISBN:978-93-5737-993-9

Email:shreeshambav@gmail.com

Web:www.shambav.org

DEDICATION

"Isavasyam idam sarvam yat kim ca jagatyam jagat, tena tyaktena bhunjitha, ma gridhah kasyasvid dhanam"

To the Almighty,

the Divine Masters,

the family who listens,

and my parents who see –

your presence shapes the pages of my life's journey.

"Isavasyam idam sarvam yat kim ca jagatyam jagat"

Meaning: "God encompasses everything you perceive, see, or touch with your sense organs."

DISCLAIMER

Living Shambavism: A Year of Inner Practice — including all six volumes (Arriving, Softening, Rooting, Abiding, Integrating, and Living) — is a contemplative work intended for personal reflection and inner exploration.

The daily passages offered throughout this year-long journey are not doctrines, commandments, or psychological prescriptions. They are invitations — gentle reflections designed to encourage awareness, presence, and thoughtful living. The structure of the books follows a natural unfolding: from stopping the search, to softening effort, to grounding awareness, to integrating presence into ordinary life. However, this progression is poetic rather than instructional. It is not a mandated sequence of development or attainment.

Shambavism, as presented here, is not a religion, therapy, or formal spiritual system. It does not replace medical, psychological, legal, or professional advice. Readers facing emotional distress, trauma, health challenges, or significant life decisions are encouraged to seek qualified professional support where appropriate.

The reflections within these volumes arise from the author's personal contemplative understanding. They are offered in good faith and with compassionate intent. Individual experiences may differ. Readers are invited to interpret and engage with the material according to their own discernment, beliefs, and lived realities.

No claims are made regarding guaranteed outcomes, spiritual attainment, psychological transformation, or measurable life results. Inner practice unfolds uniquely for each person. What resonates may be embraced; what does not may be set aside without conflict.

This series does not promote withdrawal from life, responsibilities, or relationships. On the contrary, it gently affirms presence within ordinary living — work, family, society, and the rhythms of daily existence. The later volumes especially emphasise integration, naturalness, and grounded participation in the world.

The intention of Living Shambavism is not to create dependence on a teaching, identity, or philosophy. It is to quietly point toward the reader's own awareness — already present, already functioning, already sufficient.

By engaging with these books, the reader acknowledges personal responsibility for the interpretation, application, and integration of the reflections contained herein.

May this work serve as a companion — not an authority. A mirror — not a mandate. A quiet presence — not a promise.

The journey remains your own.

Note - If any part of the book, in any sequence, hurts the reader's sentiments, it would be just out of a sheer accident not intentional

The Quiet River Within

"Move through life with a soul attuned to stillness, not the noise that clamours for attention. Hold your truths gently—live them deeply, but never wield them to wound. True strength is found not in assertion, but in understanding. Let your journey be rooted in the eternal, not fleeting acclaim. In a world chasing more, we become less—less burdened, less hardened. Like the quiet river beneath the surface, may your depth speak louder than your noise, and your silence hold the most enduring truths."

– Shree Shambav

EPIGRAM

You do not begin this book by stepping forward.
You begin by noticing that you have already arrived.
Before effort, before correction, before the urge to become more.
These pages do not lead you somewhere else.
They simply sit with you
until searching relaxes
and presence remembers itself.

– Shree Shambav

Living Shambavism

A Year of Inner Practice Volume I

Shree Shambav

Shree Shambav is a 123x best-selling author renowned for his transformative works in personal development and spiritual growth.

Dear Cherished Readers

Dear Cherished Readers,

As I embark on this new literary voyage, my heart swells with profound gratitude and an overwhelming sense of connection. With deep emotion, I extend my heartfelt appreciation to each of you who has joined me on this journey.

With sincere warmth, I invite you to revisit the steps we have taken together through the pages of my earlier works. Our odyssey began with "Journey of Soul - Karma," a book that marked my first foray into the world of words and a testament to the raw passion that ignited my writing adventure.

The subsequent chapters of our shared journey unfolded through the enchanting tapestry of the *"Twenty + One"* series. With each page turned, it felt as though a brushstroke was added to the canvas of our collective imagination—stories and sentiments woven to echo within the quiet corners of your heart. These weren't just words; they were invitations to feel, to reflect, and to remember what truly matters.

And how can I not cherish the transformative path we walked together through the *"Life Changing Journey—Inspirational Quotes Series?"* Day by day, quote by quote, we ventured inward—into spaces often overlooked—to find wisdom in simplicity and light in life's shadows. Each reflection was offered as a gentle whisper of hope, a spark meant to uplift, inspire, and remind us that even in silence, the soul speaks.

The release of "Death - Light of Life and the Shadow of Death" promises to shed new light on the timeless mystery of death.

The **Optimum Python Series** is a comprehensive learning pathway designed to empower readers at every stage of their programming journey. It begins with **Series I: Ultimate Guide for Beginners**, which builds a strong and accessible foundation in Python for newcomers. **Series II: Exploring Data Structures and Algorithms** advances into core computer science concepts, strengthening problem-solving skills and coding efficiency.

Building on this, **Series III: Python Power for Data Science** introduces powerful libraries such as NumPy, Pandas, Matplotlib, and Scikit-learn, guiding readers through data manipulation, visualisation, and foundational machine learning techniques. **Series IV: Unleashing the Potential of Data Science with**

Machine Learning Techniques explores advanced models and real-world applications.

This progression continues with **Series V: Optimum: Python Power – Unleashing the Potential of Data Science with Deep Learning Techniques**, and culminates in **Series VI: From Data to Intelligence – The Deep Learning Revolution**, enabling readers to harness the full potential of data-driven innovation. Whether you are a beginner or an advanced learner, this series serves as your complete roadmap to Python mastery and beyond.

Shree Shambav expands his artistic repertoire with *Whispers of Eternity: A Symphony of Soulful Verses*, a heartfelt exploration of the human experience expressed through lyrical depth and timeless reflection. Complementing this, his *Whispers of the Soul: A Journey Through Haiku* distils profound truths into delicate, poignant verses, capturing the fleeting essence of life with elegant simplicity.

Equally evocative, *Whispers of Stillness: Where the Soul Listens Beyond the Noise* offers meditative couplets that invite readers into a state of silence, where wisdom blossoms in the spaces between words. Together, these works illuminate Shambav's versatility and mastery of soulful expression. They invite readers on a transformative journey of self-discovery, weaving a tapestry of emotion, insight, and transcendence that lingers long after the final page is turned.

Building on this success, he continued to enchant audiences with his subsequent albums: HeartStrings, *Melodies of the Heart, Driftwood Memories, Winds of Change, The Veil and the Waves, Echoes of the Soul, Phoenix Within,* Uncaged, Where Nature Sings, and Wings of Forever. Each album further solidified his place in the world of music, offering a mesmerising collection of tracks that evoke nostalgia, introspection, and heartfelt connection. With every composition, Shree Shambav weaves a musical journey that lingers in the soul long after the final note fades.

Shree Shambav's latest works shine as luminous beacons on the path of self-discovery, mindful living, and spiritual awakening. His writings span a vast spectrum of human experience, each book offering a doorway to transformation. Among his most celebrated titles are Learn to Love Yourself: A Journey of Discovering Inner Beauty and Strength Through 10 Transformative Rules, The Power of Letting Go: Embrace Freedom and Happiness, A Journey of Lasting Peace, and The Entitlement Trap: Get Over It, Get On.

His thought-provoking works include Whispers of a Dying Soul: Unspoken Regrets and Unlived Dreams, Whispers of Silence: Unlocking Inner Power through Stillness, The Power of Words: Transforming Speech, Transforming Lives, The Art of Intentional Living:

Minimalism for a Life of Purpose, and Awakening the Infinite: The Power of Consciousness in Transforming Life.

In The Power of Manifestation: Unlocking the Path from Thought to Reality, Shree Shambav presents a transformative roadmap for turning vision into lived experience, guiding readers from intention to realisation. Beyond the Veil: A Journey Through Life After Death ventures into the profound mystery of existence beyond the physical realm, inviting contemplation on life, transition, and the eternal soul.

His other compelling works include Bonds Beyond Blood: Where Love Builds Bridges and Bonds Defy Lineage, a heartfelt celebration of love that transcends ancestry and form; The Inner Battlefield: Overcoming the Enemies of the Mind and Soul, a powerful guide to mastering inner conflicts and reclaiming mental sovereignty; and A Journey into Spiritual Maturity: 12 Golden Rules for Inner Transformation, which offers timeless wisdom for seekers evolving toward self-mastery and inner awakening.

In The Seeker's Gold: Unlocking Life's Greatest Treasure, he inspires readers to uncover the hidden riches of the soul, while The Law of Attraction: A Soulful Path reveals how to harmonise thought, energy, and intention to create a life aligned with one's highest purpose. His transformative Born to Rise series further empowers readers to embrace growth, clarity, and lasting fulfilment across every dimension of life.

Shree Shambav is also the acclaimed author of Mastering the Art of Gratitude: A Journey from Acknowledgement to Awakening, a contemplative exploration of conscious appreciation as a path to inner transformation. His poetic work, Whispers of a Silent Monk: Poetic Tales of Love, Loss, and Liberation, offers a lyrical immersion into silence, surrender, and spiritual freedom.

His visionary titles include Before We Were Born: The Sacred Stages of the Soul Before Incarnation, an inquiry into the soul's pre-earthly journey; The Architecture of Coherence: Emergence, Consciousness, and the Hidden Order Shaping Reality, a profound reflection on unity beneath complexity; When the Earth Breathes: A Shambavist Journey from Ecocide to Collective Awakening, a compassionate call for ecological and moral renewal; and The God Frequency: Shree Shambav's Vision of the One, a unifying meditation on divine oneness beyond division.

In addition, his works Journey of the Soul – Karma Unveiled, Unveiling the Enigma, and Death: Light of Life and the Shadow of Death have been translated into Gujarati and Hindi, extending his spiritual insights to a wider audience.

In addition to these works, Shree Shambav has recently ventured into astrology with the release of Astrology Unveiled – Foundations of Ancient Wisdom Series I to XIX, expanding into the realm of metaphysics. These books explore the foundational principles of Vedic astrology, offering readers a rich and practical understanding of this ancient wisdom.

Your unwavering support, enthusiasm to immerse yourself in my writings, and readiness to embark on these journeys with me have been my greatest sources of inspiration. Your input has been a beacon guiding me through the creation process, moulding these stories into containers of passion, emotion, knowledge, and resonance.

As I unveil this new narrative before you, know that your presence, insights, and shared moments have been my companions. The path we have walked together is etched in the annals of my creative evolution, and it's an honour beyond words to have you by my side once more.

Here's to the readers who have illuminated my path with their presence, who have embraced my stories with open hearts, and who have woven themselves into the very fabric of my literary world. Our journey has been a symbiotic dance of writer and reader, a harmony of souls brought together by the magic of storytelling.

With a heart brimming with appreciation and eyes glistening with anticipation, I extend my deepest gratitude for your unwavering support. Thank you for the memories, the shared emotions, and the countless hours spent in the worlds we've crafted together. As we step into this new adventure, let's continue to explore, feel, and discover the boundless horizons that words can unveil.

Warmly,

Shree Shambav

Suggested Reads

FROM BEST SELLING AUTHOR

Endorsements

Living Shambavism, Volume I offers a rare beginning—one that does not push the reader forward, but gently brings them home. These reflections dissolve the urgency to improve or progress, inviting a quiet arrival into what is already present. Read slowly, this volume becomes a daily companion for softening effort, releasing inner pressure, and rediscovering the simple dignity of being alive, just as it is.

— Dr Nita Rathod

About the Author

Shree Shambav is an internationally acclaimed best-selling author, inspirational speaker, artist, philanthropist, life coach, strategist, and entrepreneur. A world record holder, his deep passion for music led him to create soul-stirring albums, drawing inspiration from his celebrated poetry collection, Whispers of Eternity. His profound insights have sparked deep personal transformations, guiding countless individuals toward self-discovery, purposeful living, and authenticity.

With an extraordinary ability to unlock human potential, Shree empowers individuals to break through limitations and embrace their highest selves. His writings, lectures, and compassionate guidance continue to uplift lives, fostering resilience, mindfulness, and personal growth.

Shree Shambav is a 123x best-selling author celebrated for his profound contributions to personal development and spiritual growth.

Shree Shambav's literary journey took flight with the celebrated Journey of Soul - Karma, where he delved into the depths of human experience to unveil profound insights. Garnering recognition through multiple literature awards, his repertoire includes esteemed works, such as the Twenty + One Series, and the enlightening Life Changing Journey – Inspirational Quotes series.

As a distinguished alumnus of the Indian Institute of Management and the National Institute of Technology, Shree Shambav brings a wealth of corporate acumen from his tenure in multinational corporations. His most recent publications, including Unveiling the Enigma, Death - Light of Life and the Shadow of Death, and Optimum – Power Python Series I, Series II, Series III, Series IV, Series V and

Series VI, demonstrate his mastery of both the literary and technical spheres.

Shree Shambav expands his artistic repertoire with *Whispers of Eternity: A Symphony of Soulful Verses*, a heartfelt exploration of the human experience expressed through lyrical depth and timeless reflection. Complementing this, his *Whispers of the Soul: A Journey Through Haiku* distils profound truths into delicate, poignant verses, capturing the fleeting essence of life with elegant simplicity.

Equally evocative, *Whispers of Stillness: Where the Soul Listens Beyond the Noise* offers meditative couplets that invite readers into silence, where wisdom blossoms in the spaces between words. Together, these works illuminate Shambav's versatility and mastery of soulful expression. They invite readers on a transformative journey of self-discovery, weaving a tapestry of emotion, insight, and transcendence that lingers long after the final page is turned.

Building on this success, he continued to enchant audiences with his subsequent albums: HeartStrings, *Melodies of the Heart*, *Driftwood Memories*, *Winds of Change, The Veil and the Waves, Echoes of the Soul, Phoenix Within,* Uncaged, Where Nature Sings, and Wings of Forever. Each album further solidified his place in the world of music, offering a mesmerising collection of tracks that evoke nostalgia, introspection, and heartfelt connection. With every composition, Shree Shambav weaves a musical journey that lingers in the soul long after the final note fades.

Shree Shambav's latest works shine as luminous beacons on the path of self-discovery, mindful living, and spiritual awakening. His writings span a vast spectrum of human experience, each book offering a doorway to transformation. Among his most celebrated titles are Learn to Love Yourself: A Journey of Discovering Inner Beauty and Strength Through 10 Transformative Rules, The Power of Letting Go: Embrace Freedom and Happiness, A Journey of Lasting Peace, and The Entitlement Trap: Get Over It, Get On.

His thought-provoking works include Whispers of a Dying Soul: Unspoken Regrets and Unlived Dreams, Whispers of Silence: Unlocking Inner Power through Stillness, The Power of Words: Transforming Speech, Transforming Lives, The Art of Intentional Living: Minimalism for a Life of Purpose, and Awakening the Infinite: The Power of Consciousness in Transforming Life.

In The Power of Manifestation: Unlocking the Path from Thought to Reality, Shree Shambav presents a transformative roadmap for turning vision into lived experience, guiding readers from intention to realisation. Beyond the Veil: A Journey Through Life

After Death ventures into the profound mystery of existence beyond the physical realm, inviting contemplation on life, transition, and the eternal soul.

His other compelling works include Bonds Beyond Blood: Where Love Builds Bridges and Bonds Defy Lineage, a heartfelt celebration of love that transcends ancestry and form; The Inner Battlefield: Overcoming the Enemies of the Mind and Soul, a powerful guide to mastering inner conflicts and reclaiming mental sovereignty; and A Journey into Spiritual Maturity: 12 Golden Rules for Inner Transformation, which offers timeless wisdom for seekers evolving toward self-mastery and inner awakening.

In The Seeker's Gold: Unlocking Life's Greatest Treasure, he inspires readers to uncover the hidden riches of the soul, while The Law of Attraction: A Soulful Path reveals how to harmonise thought, energy, and intention to create a life aligned with one's highest purpose. His transformative Born to Rise series further empowers readers to embrace growth, clarity, and lasting fulfilment across every dimension of life.

Shree Shambav is also the acclaimed author of Mastering the Art of Gratitude: A Journey from Acknowledgement to Awakening, a contemplative exploration of conscious appreciation as a path to inner transformation. His poetic work, Whispers of a Silent Monk: Poetic Tales of Love, Loss, and

Liberation, offers a lyrical immersion into silence, surrender, and spiritual freedom.

His visionary titles include Before We Were Born: The Sacred Stages of the Soul Before Incarnation, an inquiry into the soul's pre-earthly journey; The Architecture of Coherence: Emergence, Consciousness, and the Hidden Order Shaping Reality, a profound reflection on unity beneath complexity; When the Earth Breathes: A Shambavist Journey from Ecocide to Collective Awakening, a compassionate call for ecological and moral renewal; and The God Frequency: Shree Shambav's Vision of the One, a unifying meditation on divine oneness beyond division.

In addition, his works Journey of the Soul – Karma Unveiled, Unveiling the Enigma, and Death: Light of Life and the Shadow of Death have been translated into Gujarati and Hindi, extending his spiritual insights to a wider audience.

In addition to these works, Shree Shambav has recently ventured into astrology with the release of Astrology Unveiled – Foundations of Ancient Wisdom Series I to XIX, expanding into the realm of metaphysics. These books explore the foundational principles of Vedic astrology, offering readers a rich and practical understanding of this ancient wisdom.

Shree Shambav established the Ayur Rakshita Foundation, which is dedicated to promoting boundless growth, universal fraternity, and environmental protection. The charity helps diverse communities while working for societal progress.

To learn more about Shree Shambav and his works, visit his website at www.shambhav.org. For information about the Ayur Rakshita Foundation and its initiatives, visit www.shambav-ayurrakshita.org.

Let's Follow him on Social Media: **@shreeshambav**

PREFACE

There comes a point in every sincere life when the effort to become begins to feel heavier than the desire to grow.

We strive with good intentions. We seek clarity, strength, awakening, peace. We read, reflect, practice, and refine. We attempt to correct ourselves into worthiness. And yet, beneath all improvement, a subtle exhaustion can remain — the fatigue of always moving toward something.

Living Shambavism — Volume I: Arriving was born from that exhaustion.

Not as an answer. Not as a doctrine. Not as a philosophy to adopt.

But as a resting place.

Shambavism is not a system of belief. It is not a ritual structure, nor a psychological method. It is a remembering. A quiet recognition that what we are searching for has never been absent. That awareness does not need to be constructed. That presence does not need to be achieved.

This first volume opens the year-long journey not by asking for discipline, but by inviting stillness. Before we soften, before we abide, before we live this understanding fully, we must first arrive.

Arrival, in this context, is not the completion of a long road. It is the discovery that the road was imagined. It is the gentle noticing that awareness is already functioning — breath already moving, life already expressing, consciousness already here.

For sixty days, this book offers short daily contemplations. They are intentionally simple. They do not attempt to overwhelm the mind or impress the intellect. They are meant to be encountered slowly — perhaps one each morning, or one each evening — as a quiet companion rather than a task.

You will find no dramatic promises in these pages. No guarantee of transformation. No spiritual identity to adopt. If anything shifts, it will likely be subtle. A softening of urgency. A loosening of internal pressure. A growing comfort with what is already present.

The purpose of this volume is not to elevate you. It is to relieve you.

To relieve you of the assumption that something is missing. To relieve you of the need to be elsewhere. To relieve you of the belief that you must prepare yourself for presence.

Inner practice, as offered here, does not aim at becoming extraordinary. It points toward the extraordinary simplicity of being.

You may find resistance. The mind is accustomed to movement. It prefers direction, progress, and measurable change. Arriving offers none of these. It offers quiet recognition. It invites you to sit with what has always been true.

If you move through these sixty days sincerely, something gentle may unfold. Not an achievement — but an easing. Not an identity — but a clarity. Not an arrival in time — but an arrival in awareness.

This preface is not a beginning in the traditional sense.

It is an opening of the hand.

May you enter these pages without expectation. May you read without striving. May you pause long enough to notice:

Nothing needs to change for this moment to be valid.

Welcome to Arriving.

With reverence and gratitude,

With gratitude and encouragement,

Shree Shambav

INTRODUCTION

Arriving

There is a quiet moment before any journey begins. Before intention gathers. Before improvement is imagined. Before the subtle tightening that says, I must become something more.

This book begins there.

Living Shambavism — Volume I: Arriving is not the first step on a path. It is the pause before stepping. The soft interruption of the habit of seeking. The gentle recognition that what you have been moving toward may not be ahead of you at all.

Most of life is lived in motion toward something—clarity, success, healing, awakening, completion. Even spirituality can become another form of forward-leaning effort, another promise that fulfilment waits just beyond this moment. We search not only in the world, but within ourselves. We refine, adjust, compare, and prepare.

Arriving asks something radical in its simplicity: What if you stopped?

Not stopped living. Not stopped caring. Stopped searching.

This first volume unfolds across sixty days, not as instruction, but as companionship. Each day offers a brief reflection—quiet words meant to be met lightly. They are not lessons to master or ideas to collect. There are pauses. Invitations. Mirrors.

You are encouraged to move slowly—one day at a time. No rushing ahead. No, completing the book in a single sitting. Arrival cannot be accelerated. It is not something earned through discipline or sincerity. It reveals itself when urgency relaxes.

To arrive is not to reach a destination. It is to notice that you have never left.

Nothing dramatic may occur as you read these pages. The world will remain as it is. Responsibilities will continue. Thoughts will rise and fall. Some days will feel open and clear. Others will feel ordinary or resistant. All of it belongs. Arrival does not depend on the quality of experience.

This volume gently loosens the assumption that something essential is missing. It softens the idea that you must prepare yourself for worthiness. It does not offer transcendence. It offers presence.

Breath is already happening. Awareness is already here. Life is already expressing itself as you.

Before effort. Before improvement. Before becoming someone else.

The beginning of inner practice is not striving toward a better self. It is recognising the completeness of this moment—even when it feels unfinished.

If you feel tired of seeking, this book will not ask you to try harder. If you feel restless for change, it will not promise transformation. It will sit beside you until something quieter becomes visible.

Arrival before effort. Presence before progress. Being before becoming.

This is where we begin.

Not by moving forward— but by stopping long enough to see that you are already here.

With warmth and sincerity,

Warm regards,

Shree Shambav

PROLOGUE

Living Shambavism — A Year of Inner Practice

This work did not begin as a teaching.

It began with listening.

Listening to the quiet moments that are usually overlooked.

Listening to the spaces between effort and rest, intention and outcome, seeking and surrender. Listening to life as it speaks—not in instruction, but in presence.

Living Shambavism is not a path to follow, a philosophy to adopt, or a practice to perfect. It is a year-long companionship—365 small pauses offered gently, one day at a time. Each reflection stands alone, yet together they form a slow unfolding, like the turning of seasons rather than the steps of a program.

You are not asked to change who you are here.
You are not asked to become more disciplined, more aware, or more spiritual.

Nothing in these pages needs to be completed, achieved, or understood all at once.
This work trusts something simple and often forgotten: life is already happening correctly.

Each day offers a short reflection, a quiet inner story or analogy, and a gentle invitation—not to do more, but to notice. Notice the breath that is already breathing. Notice the awareness that has never been absent. Notice the ordinariness of being alive.

Some days may feel clear.
Some days are resistant.
Some days are almost empty.

All are part of the practice—if it can even be called a practice.

You are invited to move slowly through this year. One day at a time. Not as a challenge to complete, but as a rhythm to live with. If a day is missed, nothing is lost. There is no falling behind. There is no catching up. You simply return.

The four volumes of this work mirror a natural deepening:

The first invites you to arrive.
The second allows you to move and act without strain.

The third integrates presence into responsibility and relationship.
The fourth release even the idea of practice, leaving only living.

Yet these are not stages you must pass through. They are textures of the same moment, revealed gradually, as attention softens and trust grows.

Throughout these pages, there is no promise of transcendence, no pursuit of extraordinary states. What is honoured instead is the quiet intelligence of ordinary life—how it breathes, works, loves, struggles, and rests when left unforced.

This is Shambavism.

Not the path of becoming something more, but the remembering of what has never left.

Read gently.
Listen lightly.
Let meaning arrive on its own.

Nothing here is meant to be held.
Everything here is meant to be lived.

One day.
One breath.

One ordinary moment at a time.

With reverence and gratitude.

CONTENTS

Arriving

Stopping the search.

"When the monsoon comes, it does not rush — it softens the earth the way stillness softens the heart."

- *Shree Shambav*

Day One

Arriving

You are already here.
Before effort.
Before improvement.
Before becoming someone else.

Nothing needs to change
for this moment
to be valid.

We spend much of life
trying to arrive somewhere—
a better version,
a future moment,
a finished self.

But arrival does not happen
after the journey.
It happens

when searching pauses.

Like a traveller
who suddenly realises
the destination
was never ahead…
It was the place
they were standing
all along.

Nothing dramatic happens.
The ground does not move.
The sky does not open.
Only the struggle softens.

Arrival is quiet.
It does not announce itself.
It simply notices
what is already present.

Take one slow breath.
Not to calm yourself.
Not to fix anything.
Just to notice…
that you exist.

Breath is happening.
Awareness is here.

Life has already arrived
as you.

No doorway to cross.
No preparation required.
No future moment needed
to make this one real.

Arrival is not later.
It is not earned.
It is not achieved.

Arrival
is
now.

This is Shambavism.
Not the path of becoming—
but the remembering
that you never left.

Day Two

No Goal Today

Life does not need improvement
to be meaningful.

We are taught to move forward
with targets,
with outcomes,
with something to prove.

But today
there is no finish line.
No milestone waiting.
No version of you
that needs to be reached.

A flower does not bloom
to be admired.
It does not open its petals
to be judged,

measured,
or remembered.

It blooms
because blooming
is its nature.

In the same way,
your being
requires no justification.

Action does not have to earn
a result
to be valid.
Movement does not need
a reward
to be honest.

Today,
do one small thing
without expecting anything back.

No praise.
No progress.
No outcome.
Just action
as an expression
of life moving.

Notice how ease appears
when purpose relaxes.
Notice how breath flows
when nothing is demanded.

You are not behind.
You are not lacking.
You are not unfinished.

Being
is already
enough.

This is Shambavism.
Not living to arrive—
but living
because life
is happening.

Day Three

Listen First

Before words,
there is understanding.

We are quick to speak.
Quick to explain.
Quick to respond
before the moment
has fully arrived.

But meaning does not rush.
Truth does not raise its voice.
It waits
to be received.

A still lake
reflects the sky clearly.
Clouds pass.
Light settles.
Everything is seen
as it is.

When the water is stirred,
even the sky
appears broken.
Distorted.
Unclear.

In the same way,
when the mind is busy
preparing a reply,
listening disappears.

Today,
listen without rehearsing.
Without correcting.
Without planning
what comes next.

Let words land
fully.
Let silence do
its quiet work.

Notice how presence
deepens
when response
is delayed.

Listening is not waiting

to speak.
Listening
is staying.

Listening
is presence.

This is Shambavism.
Not filling the space—
but allowing it
to speak.

Day Four

Gentle Awareness

Attention
does not have to be intense
to be true.

We often believe awareness
must be sharp,
focused,
disciplined—
something we *do*.

But awareness works best
when it is unforced.
When it arrives
without effort.

Like morning light
entering a room.
It does not push the darkness away.

It does not announce itself.
It simply appears—
and the room is seen.

In the same way,
awareness does not demand
your concentration.
It asks only
your permission.

Today,
notice your breath
once.

Not to deepen it.
Not to control it.
Not to make it meaningful.
Just to notice
that it is already happening.

See how gently
attention can rest
without strain.

Healing does not come
from intensity.
It comes from kindness.

Soft attention
heals.

This is Shambavism.
Not forcing presence—
but allowing it
to touch you.

Day Five

Let the Day Be

Resistance
adds weight
to time.

We do not suffer
because the day is heavy.
We suffer
because we push against it.

Trying to control
what has already arrived.
Arguing with moments
that are already here.

A river does not fight the land.
It does not demand
straight paths
or easier turns.

It flows
because it yields.
And in yielding,
it moves freely.

Today,
let the day be
as it is.

Not improved.
Not resisted.
Not negotiated.

Say yes
inwardly—
not as surrender,
but as a release.

Notice how time
lightens
when struggle softens.
Notice how breath
moves more easily
when nothing is opposed.

This moment
does not need your agreement
to exist.

But it relaxes
when you stop arguing with it.

Let the day be.

This moment
belongs.

This is Shambavism.
Not shaping life—
but meeting it
without resistance.

Day Six

Slow One Thing

Speed
is often fear
wearing productivity.

We rush
not because life asks us to—
but because stillness
feels unfamiliar.

Today,
nothing needs to be finished faster
to be meaningful.
Nothing needs to be completed
to be complete.

A pot watched too closely
never seems to boil.
Yet when left alone,
it warms steadily—

without pressure.

In the same way,
life unfolds
when we stop hovering over it.

Choose one small thing today—
walking,
washing,
writing,
listening—
and slow it slightly.

Not to make it sacred.
Not to improve it.
Just to feel
what happens
when time is not chased.

Notice how presence
returns
when urgency leaves.
Notice how the body
relaxes
when it is not being pushed.

Slowing
is not falling behind.

It is remembering
that you are already here.

There is time.

This is Shambavism.
Not rushing toward life—
but letting life
catch up to you.

Day Seven

Rest Without Guilt

Rest
is not a reward.
It is not something earned
after enough effort.

We are taught
to deserve rest—
after work,
after progress,
after proof.

But the body
was never designed
to justify its pauses.

A tree does not apologise
for winter.
It does not rush its leaves
back into being.

It rests
because rest
is part of growth.

In the same way,
your stillness
is not laziness.
It is intelligence.

Today,
allow one moment of rest
without explaining it.

No reason.
No permission.
No story about productivity.
Just rest
because rest is happening.

Notice how guilt
tries to speak.
Notice how it fades
when not answered.

The nervous system softens
when it realises
it is safe
to stop.

You do not fall behind
by resting.
You return
to rhythm.

Rest is not the absence of life.
It is life
repairing itself.

This is Shambavism.
Not proving your worth—
but trusting
that you already have it.

Day Eight

No Comparison

Comparison
is not observation.
It is a habit
of leaving yourself.

We are taught
to measure life—
against timelines,
against outcomes,
against other faces
walking different roads.

But existence
never asked
to be compared.

A river does not look sideways
to check its speed.
A mountain does not adjust its height
after seeing another peak.

They move
as they are.

The moon
does not compete with the stars.
It does not shine harder
to be noticed.
It reflects
what it is meant to reflect.

In the same way,
your life
needs no reference point
outside itself.

Today,
notice comparison
when it quietly appears.

Do not fight it.
Do not justify yourself.
Simply let it pass
like a thought
that was never meant to stay.

Feel how the body softens
when it stops
keeping score.

You are not late.
You are not behind.
You are not missing
someone else's life.

You are exactly
where your path
touches the ground.

No comparison
is required
for belonging.

This is Shambavism.
Not becoming more—
but remembering
you were never lacking.

Day Nine

Be With the Body

The body
never leaves
the present.

It does not wander
into yesterday.
It does not rush
toward tomorrow.
It stays
where life
is happening.

We often live
in thought—
narrating,
judging,
remembering,
anticipating.

And the body waits.

Patient.
Faithful.
Quietly here.

A house
is not understood
by thinking about it.
It is known
by standing inside it—
by feeling its walls,
its floor,
the way it holds you.

In the same way,
the body
is not an idea.
It is a place.

Today,
bring attention
downward.

Feel your feet
touch the ground.
Ten seconds.
No analysis.
No correction.
Just contact.

Notice the steadiness
already supporting you.
Notice how you are held
without effort.

Nothing mystical.
Nothing extra.
Just presence
wearing a form.

Here
is not a concept.
It is a sensation.

Here
is home.

This is Shambavism.
Not leaving the body
to find truth—
but recognizing
truth
is already embodied.

Day Ten

Speak Less

Silence
carries meaning
without effort.

We often believe
that clarity
comes from more words—
more explaining,
more defending,
more filling the space.

But truth
does not raise its voice.
It waits.

A bell
rings clearest
when struck once.
When hit again and again,
the sound blurs,

loses its edge,
forgets its shape.

In the same way,
meaning
arrives cleanly
when allowed
to echo.

Today,
notice
unnecessary words.

Not to suppress them.
Not to judge them.
Just to see
how often silence
would have been enough.

Let one sentence
end early.
Let one explanation
remain unspoken.

Notice the space
that opens.
Notice how presence
speaks

without effort.

You are not becoming smaller
by saying less.
You are becoming
clearer.

Silence is not absence.
It is precision.

Less
is clear.

This is Shambavism.
Not filling life
with sound—
but trusting
that what matters
can be heard
even in quiet.

Day Eleven

Let Feelings Pass

Feelings
are movements,
not identities.

They rise,
shift,
fade—
like weather
moving through space.

We often mistake
what passes through us
for who we are.

A moment of sadness
becomes *I am sad*.
A wave of fear
becomes *something is wrong*.

But feelings

were never meant
to stay.

Clouds pass.
The sky
remains untouched.

The sky does not argue
with a storm.
It does not hold
the rain is responsible.
It allows movement
without becoming it.

In the same way,
you are not required
to hold
what is passing.

Today,
notice one feeling
as it appears.

Name it softly—
without judgment.
Without explanation.
Without story.

Just a name.
Just recognition.

See how the body
loosens
when it is not asked
to carry meaning.

Notice how space returns
when the feeling
is allowed to move.

You are not unstable
because something stirs.
You are alive.

This is not avoidance.
It is wisdom.

What moves
will move on.

This
will move.

This is Shambavism.
Not clinging to experience—
but trusting
that awareness

is wider
than any passing state.

Day Tweleve

Simple Gratitude

Gratitude
is noticing,
not listing.

It is not a practice
of counting blessings
or convincing yourself
to feel positive.

It is the quiet recognition
that something
is already supporting you.

We often search
for reasons
to be grateful—
events,
achievements,
special moments.

But gratitude
does not depend
on decoration.

A cup
is not useful
because it is beautiful.
It serves
because it holds water.

In the same way,
life supports you
in ordinary ways
that ask
for no celebration.

Today,
notice one simple thing—
a chair,
a breath,
a window,
a moment of shade.

Do not elevate it.
Do not explain it.
Just acknowledge
that it is here
and serving its purpose.

Feel how gratitude
settles naturally
when effort relaxes.

Nothing needs
to be improved
for appreciation
to arise.

Enough
is already present.

This
is enough.

This is Shambavism.
Not chasing abundance—
but recognizing
that what is
already holds you.

Day Thirteen

Pause Before Reacting

Pause
is not hesitation.
It is space
opening.

We are trained
to respond quickly—
to defend,
to explain,
to react
before the moment
has settled.

But reaction
is often momentum,
not wisdom.

An arrow
flies straighter
when drawn calmly.

Rushed hands
shake the aim.
Still hands
know the direction.

In the same way,
clarity appears
when response
is delayed
just enough
for awareness
to arrive.

Today,
take one breath
before responding.

Not to control yourself.
Not to become polite.
Just to let the body
feel the moment
before words move.

Notice how tone softens
when breath enters.
Notice how choice appears
when urgency loosens.

The pause
does not weaken you.
It steadies you.

You do not lose power
by waiting.
You regain it.

Pause
is not silence.
It is intelligence
making room.

Pause
is power.

This is Shambavism.
Not reacting to life—
but meeting it
with space
before movement.

Day Fourteen

Be Human

Perfection
is unnecessary
suffering.

We strain
to smooth every edge.
To appear complete.
To correct what feels
unfinished.

But life
never asked
to be flawless.
It asked
to be lived.

A cracked pot
still carries water.
And through its cracks,

the path is fed.
Flowers grow
not despite the flaw—
but because of it.

In the same way,
your imperfections
are no errors.
They are openings.

We hide them.
Repair them.
Apologise for them.

But wholeness
was never the absence
of cracks.
It was the willingness
to remain open.

Today,
allow one imperfection
without correction.

A pause not polished.
A word not revised.
A feeling not fixed.

Notice how effort eases
when self-editing stops.
Notice how breath settles
when nothing needs repair.

You do not become real
by being perfect.
You become real
by being honest.

Life does not move
through ideals.
It moves
through humans.

Human
is enough.

This is Shambavism.
Not transcending humanity—
but resting
inside it.

Day Fifteen

Stay With One Moment

Life
happens
one moment
at a time.

Yet the mind
leaps ahead—
planning,
remembering,
dividing now
into many tomorrows.

Attention scatters
not because life is complex,
but because we leave
what is already here.

A candle
does not worry

about the dark corners
of the room.
It does not rush
to illuminate everything.

It shines
where it stands.
And the room
responds.

In the same way,
this moment
does not ask
for your entire life.
It asks
for your presence.

Today,
choose one simple action—
drinking,
walking,
washing,
listening.

Give it
your full attention.
Not to perfect it.
Not to make it special.

Just to let it be
the only moment.

Notice how tension softens
when the future
is not invited in.
Notice how clarity appears
when attention
is no longer split.

Life does not arrive
all at once.
It meets you
moment
by moment.

One
is enough.

This is Shambavism.
Not managing life—
but meeting it
where it is.

Day Sixteen

Quiet Kindness

True kindness
does not announce itself.

It does not wait
to be seen.
It does not ask
to be acknowledged.

We often perform goodness—
measuring its value
by response,
by recognition,
by return.

But kindness
was never meant
to be loud.

nourish the tree
unseen.
They do not display
their work.
Yet without them,
nothing stands.

In the same way,
quiet goodness
holds life together
in ways
no one applauds.

Today,
do one small act
of kindness
that no one knows about.

No witness.
No credit.
No story
to carry forward.

Just action
as care.
Just movement
as gentleness.

Notice how the heart
softens
when it is not performing.
Notice how ease appears
when goodness
is allowed
to be simple.

You do not disappear
by being unseen.
You deepen.

What nourishes quietly
lasts.

Quiet goodness
counts.

This is Shambavism.
Not proving compassion—
but living it
without announcement.

Day Seventeen

Release Hurry

Hurry
pulls you away
from yourself.

It convinces the body
that something is wrong—
that time is scarce,
that arrival is behind,
that now
is not enough.

We rush
not because life demands it,
but because the mind
fears falling behind
an invisible clock.

Yet a clock

does not rush.
Its hands move
without anxiety.
Without panic.
And time
unfolds perfectly.

In the same way,
life does not need
your urgency
to continue.

Today,
walk a little slower.

Not to resist movement.
Not to make a point.
Just to feel
how the body responds
when it is not being pushed.

Notice how breath
lengthens.
Notice how awareness
returns
when speed softens.

Hurry says

you are late.
Presence says
you are here.

Nothing essential
is missed
by slowing down.

You do not lose time
by releasing hurry.
You recover yourself.

I am not late.

This is Shambavism.
Not racing with life—
but letting it
move
with you.

Day Eighteen

Let Go of Fixing

Some things
do not need repair.
They need
acceptance.

We rush to fix—
correcting,
adjusting,
intervening—
as if discomfort
is a mistake.

But not everything
that feels wrong
is broken.

A knot
tightens
when pulled too hard.
Handled gently,

it loosens
on its own.

In the same way,
life often softens
when it is not forced
into resolution.

Today,
notice one small inconvenience.

Do not correct it.
Do not optimise it.
Do not improve it.

Let it be
slightly imperfect.

Feel the body's urge
to intervene.
Notice how it relaxes
when permission
is given
to stop fixing.

Ease appears
not because something changed,
but because resistance

did.

Acceptance
is not giving up.
It is trusting
that not everything
requires your hands.

I allow.

This is Shambavism.
Not repairing life—
but releasing
the belief
that it is broken.

Day Nineteen

Trust Your Pace

Growth
does not rush.

It unfolds
in its own rhythm,
often unseen,
often misunderstood.

We compare timelines.
We measure speed.
We wonder
why we are not further along.

But becoming
was never meant
to be hurried.

A seed
grows in darkness
long before

it breaks the soil.
Roots form.
Strength gathers.
Life prepares
without display.

In the same way,
much of your growth
is happening
out of sight.

Today,
respect your energy level.

Move when energy is present.
Rest when it is not.
Do not force
what is not ready.

Notice how the body responds
when it is trusted
instead of pushed.
Notice how ease returns
when comparison releases its grip.

You are not late.
You are not slow.
You are in season.

Nothing real
is missed
by honoring
your pace.

My pace
is right.

This is Shambavism.
Not racing toward growth—
but allowing it
to emerge
in its own time.

Day Twenty

Sit With Yourself

Your presence
is sufficient company.

We fill silence
with noise,
movement,
conversation—
as if being alone
means something is missing.

But absence
is not what appears
when others are gone.

A lamp
does not seek
another flame
to feel complete.

It shines
as it is.

In the same way,
your presence
does not require
addition.

Today,
sit quietly
for one minute.

No posture to perfect.
No thought to manage.
No insight to reach.

Just sitting.
Just being.

Notice the body
breathing on its own.
Notice awareness
resting without effort.

See how quickly
the mind searches
for distraction.
See how gently

you can return.

Aloneness
is not emptiness.
It is wholeness
without witnesses.

Nothing is wrong
with this moment.
Nothing is missing
from you.

I am here.

This is Shambavism.
Not escaping yourself—
but discovering
you were always
enough company.

Day Twenty One

Let Silence Speak

Silence
reveals
what noise
hides.

We fill space
quickly—
with sound,
with thought,
with reaction.

As if emptiness
were something
to fear.

But silence
is not empty.
It is uncovered.

Snow

falls quietly.
No announcement.
No urgency.

And yet,
by morning,
the entire landscape
is changed.

It does not argue
with the ground.
It does not explain
its purpose.

It arrives,
rests,
and transforms
without effort.

In the same way,
silence
works beneath
your noticing.

It shows
what noise
keeps hidden—
subtle feeling,

unheard truth,
unmet tenderness.

Today,
step out
of stimulation.

One minute.
No input.
No fixing.
No reaching.

Let silence
have the space
it needs
to speak.

Notice how
the mind settles
when it is not fed.
Notice how
the body listens
when nothing interrupts.

Silence
is not absence.
It is intelligence
without language.

It does not shout.
It does not persuade.

It simply knows.

Silence
knows.

This is Shambavism.
Not filling life
with answers—
but trusting
that truth
emerges
when sound
steps aside.

Day Twenty Two

Release Control

Control
tightens
life.

We hold
to plans,
to outcomes,
to the shape
we think
things should take.

As if life
were fragile
without our grip.

But control
does not protect.
It constricts.

A clenched fist

cannot
receive water.

The tighter
the hand,
the more
life slips through.

Water arrives
only
to what is open.

In the same way,
life flows
toward
relaxation.

Not because
nothing matters—
but because
trust allows
movement.

Today,
notice
where effort
is excessive.

One situation.
One moment.

Release
the urge
to manage it.

Do not correct.
Do not anticipate.
Do not brace.

Let it unfold
as it will.

Feel the body
soften
when it is not
on guard.

Notice how breath
deepens
when control
loosens.

Letting go
is not collapse.
It is cooperation
with life.

You are not
giving up.
You are
giving space.

Life does not need
to be forced
to move.

It moves
when trusted.

I trust
life.

This is Shambavism.
Not holding existence
into shape—
but allowing
what is alive
to breathe
through you.

Day Twenty Three

No Inner Violence

Harshness
does not heal.

It tightens,
shrinks,
silences.

We often speak
to ourselves
in ways
we would never
use
with another.

Correcting.
Judging.
Pressuring.
Withholding
permission
to be human.

But inner violence
leaves no visible mark.
It wounds
quietly.

You would not
shout
at a child
learning
to walk.

You would not
call them weak
for falling.
You would not
rush their balance.

You would wait.
Encourage.
Protect
their effort.

In the same way,
your becoming
does not need
force.

It needs

kindness.

Today,
notice
one critical thought
as it appears.

Do not argue with it.
Do not analyse it.

Simply
replace
the tone.

Not with praise.
Not with affirmation.

With gentleness.

One softer sentence.
One kinder breath.

Notice how the body
responds
when threat
is removed.

Safety
returns

where kindness lives.

Growth accelerates
when fear
is not driving.

You are not
made stronger
by cruelty.

You are made
steadier
by care.

I speak
gently
to myself.

This is Shambavism.
Not conquering the self—
but ending
the war
within.

Day Twenty Four

Let Joy Be Small

Joy
does not always
announce itself.

It does not require
celebration,
achievement,
or reason.

We often look for joy
in peaks—
high moments,
loud laughter,
visible success.

And miss
the quieter arrivals.

Joy often comes
softly.

A warm cup
in the hands.
A breath
that lands easily.
Light touching
the floor
just right.

A single moment
of ease.

Dew
on a leaf
reflects
the entire sky.

Nothing dramatic.
Nothing earned.
Yet nothing missing.

In the same way,
joy does not need
to be large
to be real.

Today,
notice
one small
pleasant moment.

Do not extend it.
Do not explain it.
Do not turn it
into a story.

Just let it
be felt.

Notice how the body
recognizes
what the mind
overlooks.

Joy does not ask
to be held.

It asks
to be noticed.

Small joy
matters.

This is Shambavism.
Not chasing happiness—

but allowing
what is already
here
to touch you.

Day Twenty Five

Accept the Day

Acceptance
does not mean
liking everything.

It means
stopping the argument
with what has already arrived.

Much of our effort
is not spent living the day—
but resisting it.

Pushing against
the weather of moments.
Wishing the shape of today
were different.

This resistance

adds weight
where none is required.

Acceptance
reduces
unnecessary struggle.

A door
opens more easily
when pushed
gently.

Force stiffens the hinge.
Softness finds the opening.

In the same way,
life responds
when met
without tension.

Today,
say yes
inwardly
to the day.

Not as agreement.
Not as approval.
But as an acknowledgement.

This is what is here.

Notice how energy
returns
when you stop pushing.
Notice how breath
moves
when resistance releases.

The day does not ask
for your opinion
to exist.

But it softens
when you stop
fighting its shape.

This
belongs.

This is Shambavism.
Not shaping the day—
but meeting it
as it is.

Day Twenty Six

Breathe First

Breath
steadies
what thought
disturbs.

Before reaction,
before explanation,
before movement—
there is breath.

The mind rushes ahead.
It predicts.
It prepares.
It tightens.

And the body
waits
for a signal

of safety.

Before a wave settles,
the ocean
breathes
beneath it.

The surface may be restless,
but depth
remains
undisturbed.

In the same way,
your breath
is already working
below the noise.

Today,
pause
before action.

One conscious breath.

Not to calm yourself.
Not to fix the moment.
Just to arrive
in the body
before moving.

Notice how clarity
returns
when breath leads.
Notice how urgency
loosens
when the body is consulted
first.

Breath
does not argue.
It does not hurry.
It simply
supports life
as it is.

You do not need
a better thought.
You need
contact.

Breath
is that contact.

Breath
leads.

This is Shambavism.
Not thinking your way
into balance—

but allowing breath
to set the rhythm
of response.

Day Twenty Seven

Nothing Missing

Lack
is often
forgetting.

We search
because we believe
something is absent—
a feeling,
a moment,
a piece of ourselves.

The mind learns
to scan for gaps.
To measure
what is not yet here.
To name life
as incomplete.

But existence
does not experience itself
as lacking.

A full sky
never notices
one passing cloud.

Clouds appear.
Clouds dissolve.
The sky
does not become more
or less
because of them.

In the same way,
nothing essential
has ever left you.

Today,
pause
and acknowledge
what is already present.

Three simple things.

Breath.
Ground beneath you.

Awareness itself.

Not as a gratitude practice.
Not as positive thinking.
Just recognition.

Notice how the body
softens
when it is no longer
searching.
Notice how effort
loosens
when wholeness
is remembered.

You are not incomplete
waiting to be finished.
You are complete
momentarily experiencing
movement.

Nothing needs to arrive
for this moment
to be whole.

Nothing
is missing.

This is Shambavism.

Not adding meaning
to life—
but noticing
that meaning
has never been absent.

Day Twenty Eight

End Without Judgment

Completion
does not require
evaluation.

We are taught
to review life—
what went well,
what failed,
what should have been different.

The day ends,
but the mind
keeps working.
Replaying.
Correcting.
Grading existence.

But life

does not ask
to be assessed
in order to conclude.

Night
falls
without reviewing the day.

It does not pause
to judge the light.
It does not measure
what was accomplished.
It arrives
because arrival
is natural.

In the same way,
your day
does not need
a verdict.

Today,
let the ending
be simple.

No summary.
No lesson.
No improvement plan

for tomorrow.

Just the recognition
that the day
has completed itself.

Notice how the body
unwinds
when it is not asked
to justify the hours lived.
Notice how breath
deepens
when evaluation
is released.

You do not need
to earn rest
by judging the day.
Rest arrives
when judgment ends.

Nothing needs
to be concluded
about you.

The day
can close
on its own.

I
rest.

This is Shambavism.
Not measuring life—
but allowing it
to end
without commentary.

Day Twenty Nine

Return Gently

Returning
matters more
than remembering.

The mind
will wander.
Attention
will drift.
Presence
will loosen its grip.

This is not failure.
It is movement.

We often judge ourselves
for forgetting—
for losing the thread,
for stepping away
from awareness.

But life
never asked
for constant focus.
It only invites
return.

A path
remains
even when footsteps wander.

It does not disappear
because you took
another route.
It waits—
quiet, patient,
unchanged.

In the same way,
presence
does not withdraw
when attention leaves.

It stays.

Today,
when you notice
you are distracted—
do not correct yourself.

Do not explain.
Do not apologise.

Simply
come back
to breath.

One inhale.
One exhale.
No drama.
No effort.
Just return.

Notice how the body
softens
when returning
is gentle.
Notice how awareness
feels welcoming,
not strict.

You are not required
to stay perfectly present.
You are only invited
to come back.

Again
and again—
without penalty.

Returning
is not restarting.
It is continuing
with kindness.

I
return.

This is Shambavism.
Not holding attention tightly—
but trusting
that awareness
is always
willing
to receive you.

Day Thirty

Continue

There is
nowhere else
to reach.

We are conditioned
to believe
that continuation
must lead somewhere—
a finish,
a conclusion,
a final understanding.

But life
does not move
in straight lines.
It circles.
It revisits.
It deepens
by returning.

A circle
has no beginning
and no end.

Wherever you touch it,
you are already
on the path.

In the same way,
practice
is not something
you complete.
It is something
you live.

There is no graduation
from presence.
No final day
of awareness.
No moment
when you are "done."

Only this—
continuing.

Not with effort.
Not with ambition.
But with intimacy.

Today
is not a checkpoint.
It is not a summary.
It is not an achievement.

It is simply
another moment
of being here.

Tomorrow
does not need
a plan.
It does not need
expectation.
It does not need
a better version
of you.

Begin
again—
as you are.

Notice how ease
appears
when continuation
is gentle.
Notice how the body
relaxes
when nothing

is being chased.

You are not repeating.
You are ripening.

I
continue
gently.

This is Shambavism.
Not moving toward
an end—
but walking
the circle
of being
with trust.

Arriving

The Season of Monsoon & Stillness

"Sorrow does not ask to be healed; it asks to be heard. When the heart writes what the voice cannot speak, melancholy becomes a muse, turning pain into ink and memory into meaning."

- *Shree Shambav*

Day Thirty One

The First Rain

Inward turns
restore
balance.

We are taught
to keep moving outward—
toward tasks,
toward noise,
toward response.

But the system
cannot expand forever
without drying.

There comes a moment
when turning inward
is not withdrawal—
but nourishment.

The first rain
does not flood
the land.

It softens
what has hardened.
It wakes
what has been waiting.

Dry soil
does not resist rain.
It recognises it.

In the same way,
your inward turn
is not an escape
from life.
It is a return
to balance
within it.

Today
you are not asked
to stop everything.
You are not asked
to retreat.

Only to slow

one thing.

To bring
consciousness
into a single task.

Feel how time
widens
when speed
loosens its grip.
Feel how the body
exhales
when urgency
steps aside.

This is the first rain—
not dramatic,
not overwhelming.

Just enough
to remind the land
how to breathe.

Turning inward
is not going backward.
It is how balance
renews itself.

I turn inward,

and
I am restored.

This is Shambavism.
Knowing when
to move outward—
and knowing when
to let the rain
fall quietly
inside.

Day Thirty Two

Letting the Ground Soften

Softness
allows
reception.

We often mistake
hardness
for strength.

We brace.
We tighten.
We hold ourselves
together
as if life
might break us
if we loosen.

But nothing new
can enter

what is sealed shut.

Hard soil
does not reject seeds—
it simply
cannot receive them.

Only after rain
does the ground
begin to open.

Not by force.
Not by effort.
By softening.

In the same way,
your inner resistance
is not wrong.
It once protected you.

But protection
can become a wall
long after
the danger has passed.

Today
you are not asked
to dismantle everything.

Only to notice
one place
where you are tight.
One moment
where you are braced.

And gently—
release it.

No explanation needed.
No justification required.

Feel how the reception
is not something
you do.
It is something
you allow.

Softness
is not weakness.
It is readiness.

When the ground softens,
life knows
where to enter.

Soft
is
receptive.

This is Shambavism.
Not forcing growth—
but preparing the ground
by letting
what is hard
become
kind.

Day Thirty Three

Listening to Quiet

Stillness
sharpens
awareness.

We assume
clarity comes
from more thinking,
more talking,
more response.

But the loudest parts
of the mind
are not the wisest.

Rain
does not argue
with the road.

It falls—

and the dust settles.
The echo fades.
The path
reveals itself.

In quiet,
what was always present
becomes audible.

Listening
is not an effort.
It is space.

Today
you are not asked
to be silent all day.

Only once—
pause
before responding.

Let the moment
arrive fully
before you enter it.

Notice how the body
finds its answer
before the mind

rushes to speak.

Stillness
does not slow life.
It refines it.

Like rain
quieting
even the busiest path,
silence
reveals direction
without instruction.

You do not need
to search
for clarity.

Quiet
will bring it
to you.

Quiet
clarifies.

This is Shambavism.
Learning to listen
not only
to words—
but to the space

that knows
before they form.

Day Thirty Four

Invisible Growth

True growth
does not
announce itself.

We are taught
to look
for signs—
results,
proof,
movement we can measure.

But the most important work
happens
where no one applauds.

Roots
do not seek attention.
They move
in darkness,
patiently,

without display.

The tree
does not watch them grow.
Yet it stands
because they do.

In the same way,
much of what is changing in you
cannot be seen—
not by others,
not even by you.

This is not failure.
It is depth.

Today
you are invited
to stop checking.

No measuring.
No comparing.
No wondering
if you are "there yet."

Let the work
continue
unobserved.

Notice how the body
relaxes
when it is not
being evaluated.
Notice how the mind
softens
when progress
is no longer demanded.

Growth
that is rushed
weakens.
Growth
that is trusted
stabilizes.

You do not need
to witness
your becoming.

It is already
underway.

Growth
is unseen.

This is Shambavism.
Honouring the invisible—
knowing that what deepens in darkness

will one day
support
everything above it.

Day Thirty Five

Resting the Will

Effort
relaxes
when trust
enters.

The will
is useful—
it moves,
organizes,
protects.

But when it never rests,
it hardens
into strain.

Life does not ask
for constant pushing.

Fields
do not work
while rain
falls.
They receive.
They rest.
And in that rest,
growth continues.

Effort
is not abandoned—
it is relieved
of excess.

Today
you are invited
to leave
one thing is undone.

Not as avoidance.
Not as a failure.
But as trust.

Notice what happens
when the will
steps back
and life
steps forward.

Notice how the body
unclenches
when nothing
is being forced.

Rest
is not stopping life.
It is how life
supports itself.

When the will rests,
energy returns
without demand.

You do not need
to manage everything.

Life knows
how to continue
when allowed.

Rest
supports
life.

This is Shambavism.
Letting effort soften
so trust
can take the lead.

Day Thirty Six

No Goal Today

Attention
heals
when it is
soft.

We often believe
attention must be sharp,
focused,
directed.

But healing
does not respond
to pressure.

Rain
touches everything
without force.
It does not choose.
It does not insist.
Yet nothing

is left untouched.

In the same way,
gentle attention
does not try
to fix.
It simply
meets.

Today
you are not asked
to change your breath.
Not to slow it.
Not to deepen it.

Only to notice—
once—
as it is.

See how the body
responds
when it is not corrected.
See how the system
settles
when it is not managed.

Soft attention
creates safety.

Safety
allows release.
Release
allows healing.

Nothing needs
to be forced open.
Nothing needs
to be improved.

Your presence,
when gentle,
is enough.

Soft attention
heals.

This is Shambavism.
Learning to look
without gripping—
to attend
without control—
to heal
by allowing
life
to be
as it is.

Day Thirty Seven

Allowing the Grey

Uncertainty
keeps the mind
flexible.

The mind
wants edges—
clear answers,
clean lines,
decisions it can rest on.

But life
rarely arrives
fully defined.

Clouds
do not confuse the sky.
They soften it.
They blur the edges

without losing direction.

Grey
is not a mistake.
It is a condition
of openness.

When everything
must be certain,
the mind
becomes brittle.

When uncertainty
is allowed,
the mind
can breathe.

Today
you are invited
to let one thought
remain unanswered.

No solving.
No resolving.
No forcing closure.

Notice how tension
eases

when the demand
to know
loosens.

Not knowing
is not danger.
It is space.

In that space,
new understanding
can arrive
without pressure.

You do not need
to be clear
about everything
to be at peace.

Grey
holds more wisdom
than certainty admits.

Not knowing
is
safe.

This is Shambavism.
Learning to rest
inside the unanswered—

to trust
the intelligence
of openness.

Day Thirty Eight

Strength That Bends

Flexibility
sustains
strength.

We are taught
that strength
means holding firm,
standing ground,
never yielding.

But what never bends
eventually breaks.

Bamboo
does not challenge
the storm.

It listens.
It yields.
And because it yields,
it remains.

True strength
is not rigidity.
It is responsiveness.

Today
notice one moment
where resistance
appears automatically.

Instead of tightening,
soften the response.

Not surrendering yourself—
but meeting the moment
without force.

Feel how the body
stays intact
when it does not
brace.

Yielding
is not giving up.

It is staying whole.

What bends
returns.
What resists
wears away.

You do not lose yourself
by being gentle.
You preserve yourself.

Yielding
endures.

This is Shambavism.
Learning the strength
that moves with life—
that survives storms
by knowing
when to bend.

Day Thirty Nine

Silence Working

Silence
reorganizes
the inner world.

We think
change requires effort—
attention,
analysis,
doing something right.

But there is a quieter force
at work.

Rain
does not instruct
the forest.

It falls—

and even the most restless leaves
become still.
Paths soften.
Sounds recede.
Order returns
without command.

Silence works
in the same way.

It does not argue
with the mind.
It does not fix thoughts.
It simply
gives everything
room
to settle.

Today
you are invited
to sit
in silence
for three minutes.

No technique.
No focus.
No correction.

Let silence
do
what it knows
how to do.

Notice how the system
reshapes itself
when left undisturbed.
Notice how balance
returns
without instruction.

You do not need
to manage
your inner world.

Silence
already knows
the way.

Silence
works.

This is Shambavism.
Trusting the intelligence
that operates
without effort—
the quiet force

that restores
by being.

Day Forty

Agreeing with the Day

Acceptance
lightens
time.

We spend so much energy
disagreeing—
with weather,
with schedules,
with what has already arrived.

Resistance
adds weight
to each moment.

A river
does not argue
with its bends.

It curves.
It adjusts.
And because it accepts,
it moves freely.

Life, too,
flows more easily
when not opposed.

Today
you are not asked
to like everything.

Only to stop
fighting what is.

Say yes
inwardly
to the day—
as it stands,
unfinished,
unpolished.

Notice how time
feels lighter
when it is not
being pushed against.
Notice how the body

loosens
when nothing
is being rejected.

Acceptance
does not mean
giving up your direction.
It means
walking it
without friction.

This moment
does not need
your approval.

It only asks
for agreement.

This moment
belongs.

This is Shambavism.
Moving with life
instead of against it—
letting the day
carry you.

Day Forty One

Clearing Space

Space
invites
calm
perception.

The mind mirrors
its surroundings.

When space is crowded,
attention tightens.
When space opens,
seeing softens.

A room
does not need
new furniture
to feel better.

It needs
breath.

When clutter leaves,
the room exhales.
Light travels farther.
Sound rests.
Movement becomes easy.

The same is true
inside you.

Today
you are invited
to clear
one small
physical space.

A surface.
A drawer.
A corner.

As you clear it,
notice how the body
responds—
not with effort,
but with relief.

Space
does not demand
attention.
It gives it back.

Nothing new
needs to enter.
Nothing needs
to be improved.

Simply allow
room
for what is already here
to breathe.

Space
is
relief.

This is Shambavism.
Understanding that clarity
often comes
not from adding—
but from
making space.

Day Forty Two

Waiting Well

Patience
refines
wisdom.

We often think
waiting
is empty time—
a pause between
what matters.

But waiting,
when done well,
is not inactivity.
It is preparation.

Seeds
do not rush
after rain.

They settle.
They absorb.
They wait
in the dark
until the moment
is right.

This waiting
is not hesitation.
It is intelligence.

Today
you are invited
to delay
one impulse.

Not to suppress it.
Not to judge it.

Simply
to wait.

Notice how clarity
often arrives
in the space
between urge
and action.
Notice how wisdom

forms
when time
is allowed
to do its work.

Waiting
is not falling behind.
It is ripening.

When patience enters,
understanding deepens
without effort.

You are not late.
You are not stalled.

You are waiting
well.

Waiting
ripens.

This is Shambavism.
Trusting the unseen timing—
knowing that what is ready
will rise
on its own.

Day Forty Three

Ease in Seeing

Clarity
comes
through
ease.

The mind often believes
that seeing clearly
requires effort—
focus tightened,
attention sharpened.

But clarity
does not arrive
through strain.
It arrives
when tension
releases.

Rain

does not carve the land
by force.

It smooths
sharp outlines
simply
by falling.

In the same way,
perception softens
when pressure fades.

Today
you are invited
to soften
your gaze
briefly.

Not to look away.
Not to search harder.

Just
to relax
the eyes,
the mind behind them,
the need to define.

Notice how forms

become gentler.
Notice how understanding
widens
without effort.

Ease
does not blur truth.
It reveals it.

When striving stops,
clarity steps forward
on its own.

Nothing needs fixing.
Nothing needs forcing.

Ease
reveals.

This is Shambavism.
Seeing without strain—
allowing life
to show itself
as it is.

Day Forty Four

Open Ground

Openness
nourishes
connection.

We often protect ourselves
without noticing—
tightening,
bracing,
closing small inner gates.

These defences feel safe,
but they also
limit what can enter.

An open field
does not choose
which drops to receive.

It opens
fully—
and rain
finds every inch
of ground.

Openness
is not weakness.
It is availability.

Today
you are invited
to lower
one inner defence.

Not all at once.
Not dramatically.

Just enough
to feel
a little more space
inside.

Notice what happens
when you are not guarding.
Notice how connection
forms naturally
when resistance softens.

Nothing needs forcing.
Nothing needs proving.

Life nourishes
what is open.

Openness
feeds growth.

This is Shambavism.
Living as open ground—
trusting that what arrives
is part of the nourishment
meant for you.

Day Forty Five

Enough for Today

Being
is
sufficient.

The mind often measures the day—
what was done,
what was missed,
what should have been more.

But existence
does not keep score.

Clouds
do not drift
to arrive somewhere.

They move
because moving

is natural.
They pause
because pausing
is allowed.

Nothing asks them
to justify the sky.

Today
you are invited
to drop
one self-demand.

Not to give up.
Not to retreat.

Just
to stop insisting
that you must be
something more
than what you already are
right now.

Notice the relief
that appears
when the inner pressure
loosens.
Notice how presence

deepens
when striving steps aside.

You do not need
to earn
this moment.

Breathing is enough.
Being here
is enough.

Enough
now.

This is Shambavism.
Resting inside sufficiency—
allowing the day
to complete itself
without demand.

Day Forty Six

Depth over Speed

Depth
forms
through
time.

The world rewards speed—
quick answers,
fast movement,
immediate results.

But what lasts
does not rush.

A well
does not fill
all at once.

Water gathers

slowly,
layer by layer,
until depth
is created.

Speed can impress.
Depth can sustain.

Today
you are invited
to choose
depth
over haste.

To linger
a moment longer.
To listen
before acting.
To stay
with what matters
instead of moving on.

Notice how meaning
thickens
when time
is allowed.
Notice how stability
emerges

from slowness.

There is no need
to outrun
this moment.

Depth
is already forming
beneath you.

Depth
sustains.

This is Shambavism.
Moving slowly enough
to let life
become deep.

Day Forty Seven

Let Feelings Pass

Allowed
emotions
dissolve
naturally.

Feelings often linger
not because they are strong,
but because they are resisted.

The moment judgment enters,
movement slows.

Rain
does not argue
with the valley.

It flows
through—
finding its way
without obstruction.

Emotions
are the same.

When allowed,
they move.
When blocked,
they pool.

Today
you are invited
to let
one feeling
move
without judgment.

Not to analyse it.
Not to fix it.
Not to name it
as good or bad.

Just
to feel it
as motion—

energy passing
through experience.

Notice how sensation
changes
when it is not held.
Notice how release
follows permission.

You are not required
to resolve
what is already
in motion.

This
will
pass.

This is Shambavism.
Trusting the intelligence
of emotional movement—
knowing that what is allowed
finds its own end.

Day Forty Eight

Quiet Preparation

Stillness
prepares
renewal.

What is forming
does not always announce itself.
Often,
preparation looks
like nothing
at all.

The earth
does not rush
to sprout.

It drinks
deeply—
holding moisture

in darkness
long before green appears.

Stillness
is not delay.
It is gathering.

Today
you are invited
to do
slightly less.

Not from lack.
Not from fatigue.

But from trust—
that something inside
is arranging itself
without your help.

Notice how space
creates readiness.
Notice how quiet
allows strength
to return.

You do not need
to push

the next beginning.

Preparation
is already
happening.

This is Shambavism.
Resting before renewal—
allowing life
to ready itself
in its own time.

Day Forty Nine

Trusting the Unseen

Invisible
effort
matters.

Much of what supports life
happens
where no one looks.

The mind prefers evidence—
signs,
markers,
proof of movement.

But growth
does not ask
to be witnessed.

Roots

work
without recognition.

They push through darkness,
gather nourishment,
anchor the tree—
all before anything
appears above ground.

The unseen
is not inactive.
It is essential.

Today
you are invited
to release
measuring progress.

Not to abandon care.
Not to lose direction.

Simply
to trust
that what you cannot see
is still at work.

Notice how pressure eases
when comparison drops away.

Notice how faith
forms quietly
in the absence of proof.

You are not behind.
You are not stalled.

You are rooted.

Unseen
counts.

This is Shambavism.
Honouring what works in silence—
knowing that what is unseen
is often what holds everything.

Day Fifty

Settling In

Calm
steadies
awareness.

When the inner pace slows,
attention finds its footing.

Restlessness
creates uneven ground—
thoughts rushing ahead,
the body lagging behind.

Rain
does not hurry
to level the land.

It falls
steadily,

evenly,
until sharp rises
soften
on their own.

Calm
works this way
inside.

Today
you are invited
to slow
your walking pace.

Not as an exercise.
Not as control.

Simply
as a gesture
of settling.

Feel the ground
meet each step.
Notice how awareness
spreads
when movement
is unforced.

There is no need
to arrive quickly
anywhere.

Steadiness
reveals
what speed conceals.

Steady
brings
clarity.

This is Shambavism.
Letting calm
set the rhythm—
allowing awareness
to level itself
naturally.

Day Fifty One

Signs of Renewal

Change
begins
quietly.

Not with an announcement.
Not with certainty.

Often
it begins
beneath awareness—
a soft rearranging
of something
once fixed.

Green shoots
do not break the earth
with noise.

They rise
almost invisibly—
small,
tender,
easy to miss.

Renewal
rarely shouts.
It whispers.

Today
you are invited
to notice
one subtle shift.

A softer reaction.
A slower breath.
A thought
that no longer feels
as heavy.

Do not measure it.
Do not rush it.

Simply acknowledge
that something
is moving
gently

forward.

Growth does not need
to be dramatic
to be real.

What is small
can still be true.

Renewal
whispers.

This is Shambavism.
Listening closely enough
to hear
what is already
becoming new.

Day Fifty Two

Light Returns

Energy
restores itself
naturally.

There are seasons
when everything feels dim—
heavy skies,
quiet rooms,
long pauses.

Yet even then,
nothing is broken.
Nothing is lost.

Sun
follows rain
without effort.

It does not force

the clouds to part.
It waits—
and then
it appears.

Light
is not created.
It returns.

Today
you are invited
to welcome
a lighter mood.

Not to manufacture joy.
Not to deny what was.

Simply
to notice
if something inside
feels
a little brighter.

A softer thought.
A clearer breath.
A quiet readiness.

Do not question it.

Do not analyse it.

Let the warmth
be simple.

Energy knows
how to renew itself
when given space.

Light
returns.

This is Shambavism.
Trusting the rhythm
of dimness and brightness—
knowing both belong
to the same sky.

Day Fifty Three

Grounded Balance

Balance
rebuilds
trust.

When everything feels tilted,
the mind searches
for something
to hold.

But balance
does not come
from tightening.
It comes
from settling.

Soil
shifts
after rainfall.

Water moves through it,
softens it,
rearranges it—
and then
the ground
becomes firm again.

Not rigid.
Just steady.

Balance
is quiet stability.

Today
you are invited
to feel
your feet
on the earth.

Not symbolically.
Physically.

Notice the contact.
Notice the support
already beneath you.

The ground
does not rush.

It does not lean.
It simply
holds.

Let your breath
descend.
Let your weight
settle.

Trust returns
when the body
feels supported.

Grounded
is stable.

This is Shambavism.
Standing where you are—
allowing balance
to rebuild itself
from the ground up.

Day Fifty Four

Emerging Clarity

Clarity
unfolds
gradually.

The mind prefers
immediate answers—
sharp edges,
clear lines,
final conclusions.

But understanding
rarely arrives
all at once.

Mist
does not vanish
because it is ordered to.

It lifts

slowly—
revealing shapes
as light
increases.

Nothing is forced.
Nothing is hurried.

What was hidden
becomes visible
in its own time.

Today
you are invited
to wait
before deciding.

Let the first reaction
settle.
Let the second thought
soften.

Give space
for something deeper
to rise.

Notice how patience
changes perception.

Notice how quiet
clarifies
without pressure.

You do not need
to push
for certainty.

Clarity
ripens.

This is Shambavism.
Trusting the slow reveal—
allowing understanding
to emerge
like morning light
through thinning mist.

Day Fifty Five

Gentle Consistency

Gentle effort
endures.

Intensity
can begin quickly—
bright,
strong,
impressive.

But what sustains
is rarely loud.

Saplings
do not force
their height.

They grow
steadily—
a little each day,

roots deepening
while branches
reach quietly upward.

No strain.
No display.
Just continuity.

Consistency
does not mean pressure.
It means return.

Today
you are invited
to do
one thing
carefully.

Not perfectly.
Not quickly.

Just
with attention.
With steadiness.
With care.

Notice how gentleness
changes the quality

of action.
Notice how calm effort
feels sustainable.

There is no need
to push growth.

Small, steady movement
shapes lasting strength.

Gentle
lasts.

This is Shambavism.
Returning again and again—
without force,
without rush—
trusting that steady care
builds what endures.

Day Fifty Six

Inner Rhythm

Your rhythm
knows
the way.

The world moves
in schedules—
deadlines,
alarms,
measured hours.

But beneath that structure
there is
another timing.

Rain
does not consult
the clock.

It gathers,

waits,
and falls
when the air
is ready.

Too early,
and it withholds.
Too late,
and it passes.

Its rhythm
belongs
to something deeper
than urgency.

You have
this rhythm
within you.

A natural pace
for speaking.
For resting.
For creating.
For deciding.

Today
you are invited
to honor

your natural pace.

Notice when you speed up
to match expectation.
Notice when you slow
because it feels true.

Let your breath
set the tempo.
Let your body
confirm it.

There is wisdom
in timing
that feels aligned.

Trust
rhythm.

This is Shambavism.
Living in tune
with your own cadence—
allowing life
to unfold
in the timing
that fits you.

Day Fifty Seven

Quiet Strength

Strength
forms
inwardly.

It is not always visible.
Not always loud.
Not always declared.

The strongest structures
are often
supported
by what cannot be seen.

Roots
anchor
tall trees.

They spread in darkness,

pressing into earth,
holding steady
against wind
long before branches
ever sway.

The tree does not announce
its stability.
It simply stands.

Quiet strength
does not argue.
It does not defend
its presence.

It rests
in knowing.

Today
you are invited
to stand firm
without explanation.

No need
to justify your calm.
No need
to prove your position.

Let your stillness
be enough.
Let your groundedness
speak without words.

Strength deepens
when it is not displayed.

Strength
is rooted.

This is Shambavism.
Growing downward
as much as upward—
trusting that what anchors you
does not require
attention
to be real.

Day Fifty Eight

Whole Attention

Presence
completes
action.

Many tasks
are started
with divided focus—
the mind ahead,
the body behind.

Attention scattered
leaves something unfinished,
even when the task is done.

Rain
finishes
the field's work.

It settles dust,
fills the soil,
touches every corner
without omission.

Nothing partial.
Nothing withheld.

Whole attention
is like this.

When you are fully here,
what you do
feels complete—
even if small.

Today
you are invited
to be fully present
in one task.

Washing.
Walking.
Writing.
Listening.

Let your awareness
rest entirely

on what is in front of you.

Notice how simplicity
deepens.
Notice how effort
softens.

Completion
is not about finishing more.
It is about arriving fully.

Here
is whole.

This is Shambavism.
Gathering attention
into the moment—
allowing presence
to complete
what you begin.

Day Fifty Nine

Absorbing Growth

Stillness
integrates
change.

Growth is not only
movement forward.
It is also
settling in.

After effort,
after insight,
after emotion—
there is a quiet phase
where everything
finds its place.

Earth
settles

after a long rain.

Water sinks deeper.
The surface softens.
The ground reshapes
itself slowly.

Nothing dramatic.
Nothing visible.
Yet everything
is adjusting.

You, too,
need this pause.

Today
you are invited
to rest
without guilt.

Not as avoidance.
Not as delay.

But as integration.

Let the body be still.
Let the mind unclench.
Let experience

absorb
into understanding.

There is wisdom
in stopping.
There is strength
in allowing
what has shifted
to settle.

Integration
happens.

This is Shambavism.
Trusting that stillness
is not stagnation—
it is the quiet work
of becoming whole.

Day Sixty

Roots Established

Inward work
prepares
outer movement.

Before visible change,
there is quiet preparation.
Before forward steps,
there is unseen grounding.

Growth does not begin
at the surface.
It begins
below.

After monsoon,
fields stand ready.

The rain has soaked deep.

The soil has absorbed
what it needed.

Nothing appears dramatic—
yet everything
is prepared.

Strength has gathered
where eyes cannot see.

You, too,
have been growing
beneath the surface.

Lessons absorbed.
Patience practised.
Silence endured.
Trust rebuilt.

Today
you are invited
to acknowledge
your inner depth.

Not to display it.
Not to measure it.

Simply to recognise

that roots
have formed.

Stand gently.
Breathe steadily.
Feel the quiet foundation
within you.

Movement will come
when it is time.

For now,
know this—
roots
are deep.

This is Shambavism.
Honouring the unseen work
that prepares the path—
trusting that what anchors you
makes every future step
steady.

Life Coach and Philanthropist

Shree Shambav is the visionary founder of the Shree Shambav Ayur Rakshita Foundation (www.shambav-ayurrakshita.org). He founded this institution with a lofty goal: to recognise human identity across gender, ethnicity, and nationality. Through this organisation, he wants to assist all communities in realising their full potential and the intrinsic beauty of life.

Shree Shambav, a Life Coach, is dedicated to supporting people on their journeys of self-discovery and empowerment. He assists people in discovering who they are, determining what inspires and drives them, and overcoming limiting ideas. His approach clarifies what one wants in life, assisting people through goal-setting and a step-by-step process for achieving them. He empowers people to make deliberate and responsible decisions, allowing them to identify their blind spots and evolve as individuals via the use of numerous strategies and tools.

The foundation's bold, uncompromising, and compassionate ventures are always aimed at initiating the "Inner Transformation" process. They focus on spiritual growth, personal growth, and self-healing while emphasising that true progress lies in "Inclusive Growth and Co-existence." This philosophy drives all their initiatives, encouraging a holistic approach to development and well-being.

Under Shree Shambav's leadership, the foundation has launched several impactful movements:

Shree Shambav Green Movement: This mission is to create a healthy, green, and clean earth through responsible water conservation and greening initiatives. The movement strives to make the world a green paradise by encouraging sustainable living and environmental responsibility.

Shree Shambav Vidya Vedhika (Vizhuthugal): This project aims to help students and children by offering training, books, stationery, and uniforms. It aims to provide the next generation with the tools and resources they need to excel both academically and personally.

Shree Shambav and his foundation exemplify the spirit of compassion, transformation, and inclusive growth via their work, which has a profound impact on individuals and communities around the world. His work exemplifies the power of acknowledging and nourishing the human spirit, creating a world in which everyone can reach their full potential and appreciate the beauty of life.

TESTIMONIALS

Journey of Soul - Karma - "We die in our twenties and are buried at eighty." Remember that nothing can stop someone who refuses to be stopped. "Most people do not fail; they simply give up." Shree Shambav deserves full credit. It allowed me to sit and consider what I might miss out on in life. The author has delved into every aspect of our daily lives. How can a seemingly insignificant change in these seemingly insignificant details bring us such joy? The Soul of Journey teaches you the "art of living" as well as the "art of dying."

Twenty + One Series - The rich cultural heritage offered a host in twenty + one short stories with incredible imagination, morals and values prevalent at a given time, influencing how people respond to a crisis or any situation. The author has recreated images with universal values and morals. The plentiful of fascinating from faraway lands would leave the modern play and story writers a cringe. The book supports trust and immeasurable values instilling hope for the new generations.

Death - "Shree Shambav's 'Death - Light of Life and the Shadow of Death' is an extraordinary masterpiece that delves deep into the profound questions surrounding our existence and mortality. The book's opening statement, 'Nothing ever truly dies; it simply ceases to exist in one form before resuming it in another,' sets the stage for a thought-provoking exploration of death's multifaceted nature. Shambav's remarkable ability to navigate the philosophical complexities of death and our universal fear of it is both enlightening and comforting. This book is a testament to the power of understanding and acceptance."

Whispers of Eternity - "Reading 'Whispers of Eternity' by Shree Shambav was a transformative experience that left me captivated from beginning to end. Each section of this exquisite collection delves into the myriad facets of existence, offering poignant reflections on life, death, and everything in between. Shree Shambav's verses are a testament to the beauty of language and the power of expression, inviting readers to embark on a journey of self-discovery and spiritual awakening. Whether celebrating life's simple joys or grappling with the complexities of human emotion, this book is a timeless companion that speaks to the heart and soul of every reader."

Life Changing Journey Series - "Life Changing Journey Series II Inspirational Quotes" is a remarkable collection that illuminates the path to self-discovery and personal growth. With its inspiring quotes and insightful reflections, this book serves as a beacon of light in a world often shrouded in darkness. Each quote offers wisdom, guidance, and encouragement, reminding readers of their inner strength and resilience. A must-read for anyone seeking inspiration and enlightenment.

Learn To Love Yourself – "A Heartfelt Guide to Authentic Self-Love." "Learn to Love Yourself" invites readers on a transformative journey to embrace their true essence in a world often focused on external validation. Through ten insightful chapters, it gently reveals principles of genuine self-love, guiding readers to deepen their connection with themselves. Beyond surface positivity, it encourages the cultivation of resilient self-acceptance, from embracing one's unique qualities to setting empowering boundaries. With inspiring stories and practical wisdom, this book is a trusted companion on the path to inner peace, fulfilment, and joy, helping readers build lives that reflect their authentic selves.

The Power of Letting Go – This book has been a gift to my spiritual journey. Shree Shambav's insights into attachment, personal growth cycles, and forgiveness are enlightening. The concept of seven-year cycles resonated with me, helping me understand the natural phases of life. I feel more empowered to let go of what no longer serves me and step into a life of freedom and fulfilment. A truly beautiful read!

A Journey of Lasting Peace – "A Journey of Lasting Peace" feels like a trusted friend guiding you through the maze of self-discovery. The 18 transformative principles are both practical and deeply resonant, addressing everything from gratitude practices to the art of letting go. Each chapter is infused with warmth and wisdom, making it easy to apply the concepts to my life. I particularly appreciated the emphasis on physical health's connection to mental well-being; it served as a wake-up call for me to prioritise my health. This book is an invaluable resource for anyone serious about personal growth!

Astrology Unveiled Series – "Profound, Logical, and Inspiring". What stands out in Astrology Unveiled is the author's dedication to making Vedic astrology logical and approachable. Each concept flows naturally into the next, backed by examples and exercises. The insights into karma and life cycles add a philosophical depth rarely seen in astrology books.

Perfect for anyone seeking spiritual growth alongside astrological knowledge!

The Entitlement Trap - "Thought-Provoking and Challenging" The book challenges readers to confront their own sense of entitlement, and that's not easy—but it's essential. The Entitlement Trap doesn't offer a one-size-fits-all approach. Instead, it's a thoughtful, layered examination of how entitlement can limit our growth. The chapter on "Defining Your Own Hill" was particularly impactful, as it pushed me to reconsider which challenges are truly worth pursuing. A thought-provoking read for those willing to do the inner work to create a life they can be proud of.

Whispers of a Dying Soul – "A Soul-Stirring Reflection on Life's Unspoken Truths" **-** *Whispers of a Dying Soul: Unspoken Regrets and Unlived Dreams"* is a deeply moving exploration of the unexpressed emotions and unfulfilled aspirations that shape our lives in ways we often don't realise. This book invites readers to confront the powerful, often hidden impact of regret while guiding them through a journey of introspection and healing. Each page opens a space to reflect on the choices that define us—from moments of unspoken love to neglected passions—offering a gentle reminder to live authentically and courageously.

Whispers of the Soul: A Journey Through Haiku - is a mesmerising collection that speaks directly to the heart. Each haiku is a delicate brushstroke capturing life's fleeting beauty and timeless wisdom, inviting readers into moments of deep reflection and peace. This book is a balm for the soul, guiding us to find meaning in stillness and connection in simplicity. The themes of nature, love, and mindfulness echo universal truths, resonating with quiet, powerful grace. It's a book to be savoured slowly, cherished deeply, and returned to often. Truly, a gift for anyone seeking calm and clarity in life's chaos.

Whispers of Silence - Unlocking Inner Power through Stillness by Shree Shambav is a rare gem that beckons readers to pause, reflect, and reconnect with their inner selves. In a world that never stops talking, this book offers a profound exploration of silence—not as a void but as a rich and transformative space.

From the first page, Shree Shambav's writing resonates deeply, blending scientific insights with spiritual wisdom in a way that feels both universal and deeply personal. The author's ability to bridge the tangible and the transcendent makes this book an invaluable guide for anyone navigating the chaos of modern life.

The Power of Words: Transforming Speech, Transforming Lives - "The Power of Words is a profound and enlightening guide that has transformed the way I approach communication. Shree Shambav masterfully uncovers the hidden influence of our words on relationships, self-perception, and overall well-being. This book doesn't just teach you how to speak; it inspires mindful communication that fosters connection and trust. The insights on replacing negative patterns like gossip and judgment with kindness and authenticity are truly life-changing. The practical strategies and engaging narratives make it an invaluable resource for personal and professional growth. A must-read for anyone striving to communicate with intention, clarity, and compassion. Highly recommended!"

The Art of Intentional Living: Minimalism for a Life of Purpose - "The Art of Intentional Living is a refreshing guide to finding clarity in a cluttered world. With practical wisdom and profound insights, it inspires you to simplify, prioritise, and live with purpose. A must-read for anyone seeking balance and fulfilment."

Awakening the Infinite: The Power of Consciousness in Transforming Life - "Awakening the Infinite is a transformative guide that expands the mind and nourishes the soul. With profound insights and practical wisdom, this book beautifully explores the power of consciousness, helping readers connect with their true purpose and inner potential. It is a journey of self-discovery, healing, and spiritual awakening, offering clarity and inspiration at every turn. A must-read for anyone looking to live with greater awareness, meaning, and authenticity."

Beyond the Veil: A Journey Through Life After Death:

"This book touched me in ways few others have—it's not just about death, but about life, meaning, and the vast unknown that connects them. Beyond the Veil offers a graceful blend of science and spirit, inviting us to explore the mystery with awe rather than fear. The stories, insights, and reflections linger in your heart long after the final page. A truly transformative read that brings light on the shadows of mortality. It reminded me that in embracing death, we truly learn how to live."

Bonds Beyond Blood:

"A profoundly moving story that reminds us, family is not defined by blood, but by love, sacrifice, and the courage to heal. Every chapter touched my soul with its emotional truth and timeless wisdom. Through joy, grief, and redemption, this book captures the raw beauty of human connection. I saw reflections of my own family in its pages—both the pain and the hope. A powerful, unforgettable read that lingers long after the final word."

A Journey into Spiritual Maturity: 12 Golden Rules for Inner Transformation

"This book is a gentle yet powerful guide that awakened a deeper sense of purpose within me. Each golden rule felt like a mirror reflecting truths I needed to embrace. Shree Shambav's wisdom is timeless, poetic, and profoundly grounding. It's not just a read—it's a journey into the heart of who you truly are. A must-read for anyone seeking lasting peace, clarity, and inner transformation."

The Inner Battlefield: Overcoming the Enemies of the Mind and Soul:

"This book is a powerful revelation—an honest mirror to the battles we fight within. Every chapter is a step closer to clarity, peace, and emotional mastery. Shree Shambav brilliantly transforms ancient wisdom into practical guidance for modern souls. It awakened in me a new strength to face my fears and rise above inner turmoil. A must-read for anyone seeking true inner victory and lasting transformation."

The Seeker's Gold – Unlocking Life's Greatest Treasure

The Seeker's Gold is a soul-stirring masterpiece that goes far beyond the pursuit of wealth—it is a journey into the heart of what truly matters. Each chapter unfolds with poetic wisdom and emotional depth, revealing that life's real treasure is not found in riches but in the transformation of the self. As the protagonist evolves through trials, love, and profound realisations, so does the reader. This book is a mirror for every dreamer, a lantern for every seeker, and a companion for anyone walking the path of purpose. A timeless tale that stays with you long after the final page.

Born to Rise Series I & II:

Born to Rise – Series I & II is a profound awakening—a journey that begins in silence and leads you to the core of your true power.

Series I reshapes your understanding of success, showing that clarity is more valuable than applause, and authenticity more powerful than performance.

Series II takes you deeper, unlocking the mindset and inner strategy behind meaningful, lasting growth—not just in wealth, but in wisdom.

Together, these books are not just guides—they are soul mirrors, revealing the truths you've forgotten and the strength you've always held.

This is more than reading—it's remembering who you are, and rising with purpose, not pressure.

The Law of Attraction: A Soulful Path:

The Law of Attraction: A Soulful Path is more than a guide—it's a spiritual companion. Shree Shambav has beautifully woven timeless wisdom with practical tools, helping me understand that manifestation isn't about control—it's about inner alignment and grace. Each rule in this book felt like a key unlocking something dormant within me. I've read many books on the Law of Attraction, but none touched my heart like this one. Through soulful rituals, deep reflection, and gentle encouragement, I began releasing old fears and stepping into clarity and peace. This book helped me move from desperation to trust, from wanting to becoming. It's a must-read for anyone yearning for meaning, healing, and true, lasting transformation.

Whispers of Stillness: Where the soul listens beyond the noise Series:

Whispers of Stillness is a rare and luminous work that speaks softly yet transforms deeply. Each couplet feels like a breath of wisdom—gentle, precise, and profoundly awakening. Moving gracefully through Virtue, Wealth, and Love, the series invites quiet reflection, ethical clarity, and emotional truth. This is not poetry to rush through, but to live with. A timeless companion for seekers, leaders, and sensitive hearts, it restores stillness where the soul can truly listen.

Mastering the Art of Gratitude:

Mastering the Art of Gratitude is not a book you simply read—it is a journey you live. Across its three beautifully woven volumes, gratitude transforms from a polite emotion into a steady, luminous way of being. The writing is lyrical yet deeply grounded, blending spiritual insight, psychology, and reflective practice with rare grace. Each page invites slowing down, softening resistance, and seeing life—joy and sorrow alike—as sacred teachers. What touched me most is how gratitude becomes embodied, practical, and sustaining through real challenges. This series doesn't teach gratitude; it awakens it within you, gently and lastingly.

The Power of Manifestation:

The Power of Manifestation reshaped how I understand creation itself. This book moves far beyond wishful thinking, revealing manifestation as conscious alignment between thought, emotion, energy, and action. With clarity and depth, it bridges ancient wisdom, quantum science, and soulful introspection into a path that feels both grounded and expansive. What stood out most is its emphasis on inner responsibility—manifestation not as control, but as harmony with life's flow. The practices are practical, the insights profound, and the tone deeply compassionate. This is not about chasing outcomes, but becoming the kind of being from which aligned realities naturally arise.

Whispers of a Silent Monk:

Whispers of a Silent Monk is a rare and tender literary offering that speaks directly to the heart. Through poetic tales and quiet parables, this series reminds us that true wisdom does not shout—it arrives softly, like breath or prayer. Each story feels timeless, gently exploring love, loss, grief, and liberation without preaching or prescription. The monk's presence is compassionate and human, revealing how everyday moments carry sacred meaning. These books invite stillness, reflection, and deep listening in a noisy world. Reading them feels less like consuming words and more like walking slowly beside truth itself, one whisper at a time.

Before We Were Born:

Before We Were Born is a quietly powerful series that reshapes how you see life itself. Rather than offering beliefs, it invites remembrance—revealing existence as a consciously chosen journey of awakening. Through poetic dialogue and deep stillness, suffering becomes initiation, karma becomes intelligence, and birth becomes an act of courage, not loss. What moved me most is the gentle responsibility it restores: life is not random, yet never guilt-bound. Each page feels less like reading and more like recognition, as if truths long known are being softly uncovered. This is not a book that tells you who you are—it reminds you why you came.

When the Earth Breathes:

When the Earth Breathes is a deeply moving and necessary work for our times. It does not argue or alarm—it awakens. Through poetic wisdom and lived insight, the series restores the Earth as a living presence rather than a resource to be managed. What makes these volumes extraordinary is how seamlessly they unite ecology, spirituality, and inner responsibility. Environmental destruction is revealed not as a technical failure, but as a forgetting of relationship. Reading this feels like listening to the planet itself—quiet, patient, and truthful. It leaves you not with fear, but with reverence, resolve, and a renewed sense of belonging within the living world.

The Architecture of Coherence:

The Architecture of Coherence is one of the most intellectually satisfying and quietly transformative works I've encountered. It bridges science, philosophy, consciousness, and society with rare clarity, showing how meaningful wholes arise—and why some endure while others collapse. What makes this book exceptional is its refusal of both reductionism and mysticism, offering instead a grounded vision of emergence rooted in structure, relationship, and constraint. From physics to ethics, consciousness to civilisation, each insight builds with coherence itself. This is not abstract theory for specialists alone; it reshapes how you see systems, responsibility, and meaning. Reading it feels like learning how reality holds together—and how we might too.

ACKNOWLEDGEMENTS

To my grandfathers, grandmothers, mothers, fathers, aunts, uncles, neighbours, sisters, brothers, friends, and teachers, they poured in endless moral stories, retellings of Ramayana, Mahabharata, Puranas, Upanishads, and so on.

My teachers, neighbours, and kindred souls. Who provided us with a stage to perform wonderful Puranic stories and were gracious enough to acknowledge our efforts.

The artists and translators of epics have served as a source of inspiration, invigorating our spirits, making these works accessible, and enabling us to grasp the profound depths and deeper dimensions they contain.

I also cherish the stimulating conversations; I had with my wonderful mothers, Punitha Muniswamy and Uma Devi.

Our family's youngest member, Aadhya, who always overwhelmed me with questions, inspired this book.

I would likewise prefer to express gratitude to Mr Sivakumar, Mrs Roopa Sivakumar, Mr Akshaya

Rajesh, Ms Akshatha Rajesh, Ms Apeksha Prabhu, Mr Akanksh Prabhu, Mr Nikash Sarasambi, and Mrs Spoorthi Nikash for their valuable inputs.

I must thank Mr Rajesh, Mr Savan Prabhu, Mrs Revathi Rajesh, Mrs Rajani Sarasambi, and Mrs Manju Reshma, who encouraged me and often suggested writing a book. Their unwavering belief that I had something valuable to offer kept me going during my writing sessions.

Love you all,

Shree Shambav

www.shambav.org

shreeshambav@gmail.com

9 789357 379939

Printed at Repro India Ltd.